Fort Sumter
Anvil of War

Fort Sumter National Monument
South Carolina

Produced by the
Division of Publications
National Park Service

U.S. Department of the Interior
Washington, D.C. 1984

About This book
Early on the morning of April 12, 1861, a mortar
shell fired from Fort Johnson in Charleston Harbor
burst almost directly over Fort Sumter, inaugurating
the tragic American Civil War. Two years later, Fort
Sumter, now in Confederate hands, became the focus
of a gallant defense in which determined Confederate soldiers kept Federal land and naval forces at
bay for 587 days. The "first shot" of 1861 and the
Confederate defense of 1863-65 are the subjects of
the following pages. The narrative is based on an
earlier work by Frank Barnes, onetime historian at
Fort Sumter National Monument.

National Park handbooks, compact introductions
to the natural and historical places administered by
the National Park Service, are designed to promote
public understanding and enjoyment of the parks.
Each handbook is intended to be informative read-
ing and a useful guide to park features. More than
100 titles are in print. They are sold at parks and
can be purchased by mail from the Superintendent
of Documents, U.S. Government Printing Office,
Washington, DC 20402.

Library of Congress Cataloging in Publication Data:
Fort Sumter: anvil of war
    Bibliography: p.
    Supt. of Docs. no. : I 29.9/5:127
    1. Fort Sumter (Charleston, S.C.)—History. 2.
Charleston, (S.C.)—History—Civil War, 1861-1865.
3. Charleston, (S.C.)—Fortifications, military instal-
lations, etc. 4. Fort Sumter National Monument
Charleston, (S.C.) I. United States. National Park
Service. Division of Publications.
F279.C48F684 1984   975.7'915   84-600248

ISBN 0-912627-24-7

Part 1

The Fort on the Shoal

The Fort on the Shoal

*Kentucky-born Maj. Robert Anderson had never seen Fort Sumter before November 1860, when he was sent to command the Federal forts in Charleston Harbor as the secession crisis mounted. His honorable defense of Fort Sumter in April 1861 made him a national celebrity and linked his name more closely to the place than anyone else's, including those who planned and spent so many years building it. The painting shows Anderson inside Fort Moultrie, where he was headquartered upon his arrival in Charleston. Fort Sumter lies in the distance. **Previous pages:** Fort Sumter on the eve of the Civil War as painted by Seth Eastman. For Eastman's companion view of Sumter at the close of the war, see pages 50-51.*

". . . the character of the times particularly inculcates the lesson that, whether to prevent or repel danger, we ought not to be unprepared for it. This consideration will sufficiently recommend to Congress a liberal provision for the immediate extension and gradual completion of the works of defense, both fixed and floating, on our maritime frontier. . . ."

—President James Madison to Congress, December 15, 1815.

Anyone visiting Fort Sumter today will find it difficult to believe that it could ever have ranked among the "most spectacular harbor defense structures to come out of any era of military architecture." Wrecked by the Civil War, its walls reduced to half their original height, the present fort only slightly resembles the huge fortification that dominated the entrance to Charleston Harbor in the middle years of the 19th century.

Fort Sumter was one of a series of coastal fortifications built by the United States after the War of 1812—a war that had shown the gross inadequacy of American coastal defenses. The fort belonged to what has come to be known as the Third American System of coastal defense, embodying "structural durability, a high concentration of armament, and enormous overall firepower." This system emerged after Congress set up a military Board of Engineers for Seacoast Fortifications in answer to President Madison's plea.

Under the unofficial direction of Brig. Gen. Simon Bernard, onetime military engineer to the emperor Napoleon I, the Board began surveying the entire coastline of the United States in 1817. The South Atlantic coast, "especially regarded as less important," was not surveyed until 1821. One fortification report, covering the Gulf coast and the Atlantic coast between Cape Hatteras and the St. Croix River, had been submitted to Congress earlier that year, but it

Fort Sumter on the Eve of War

When Federal troops occupied Fort Sumter in late December 1860, they found the place "filled with building materials, guns, carriages, shot, shell, derricks, timbers, blocks and tackle, and coils of rope in great confusion." The soldiers spent many weeks clearing away debris, moving and mounting guns, distributing shot, and bricking up embrasures against a threatened Confederate attack. By April 1861 the fort looked much as it does below.

The principal parts of the 1861 fort are identified in the following list. Each is keyed by number to the illustration. The cutaway section of the illustration shows the arched first- and second-tier casemates behind the brick exterior. The second-tier casemates were unfinished and no cannon were mounted there.

1/**Left Face**
2/**Left Flank,** facing Charleston and Fort Johnson.
3/**Right Face,** fronting Fort Moultrie across the main ship channel.
4/**Right Flank,** facing the Atlantic Ocean.
5/**Gorge Wall,** facing Confederate batteries on Morris Island.
6/**Left Gorge Angle**
7/**Right Gorge Angle,** where Capt. Abner Doubleday commanded a Federal gun crew in one of the lower casemates.
8/**Officers' Quarters,** consisting of several three-story

apartments for officers and their families. Ordnance storerooms and a hospital were also located here.
9/**Enlisted Men's Barracks,** each designed to accommodate two companies.
10/**Stair Tower,** providing access to the barbette tier.
11/**Hot Shot Furnace**
12/**Second Tier Embrasures**
13/**Fort Lantern**
14/**Bins** containing oyster shells probably used in the fort's construction.
15/**Sand and Brick-bat Traverses,** erected by Federal engineers as protection

against Confederate cannon fire.
16/**Sandbag Traverse,** built to protect Federal gunners against enfilading fire from Fort Moultrie.
17/**Machicoulis Gallery,** a wooden outcropping atop the parapet in which soldiers could stand to fire into or drop grenades onto an attacking force.
18/**Sally Port**
19/**Granite Wharf**

was not until the revised form of the report appeared in 1826 that much thought was given to permanently occupying the shoal in Charleston Harbor opposite Fort Moultrie. If the location were feasible, the Board reported, "the fortification of the harbor may be considered as an easy and simple problem." With the guns of the projected fort crossing fire with those of Fort Moultrie, the city of Charleston would be most effectively protected against attack.

Plans for Fort Sumter were drawn up in 1827 and adopted on December 5, 1828. In the course of that winter Lt. Henry Brewerton, Corps of Engineers, assumed charge of the project and commenced active operations. But progress was slow, and as late as 1834 the new fort was no more than a hollow pentagonal rock "mole" two feet above low water and open at one side to permit supply ships to pass to the interior. Meanwhile, the fort had been named Sumter in honor of Thomas Sumter, brigadier general commanding South Carolina militia during the Revolution.

Operations were suspended late in the autumn of 1834 when ownership of the site came into question. The previous May, one William Laval, a resident of Charleston, had secured from the State a rather vague grant to 870 acres of "land" in Charleston Harbor. In November, acting under this grant, Laval notified the representative of the U.S. Engineers at Fort Johnson of his claim to the site of Fort Sumter. In the meantime, the South Carolina Legislature had become curious about the operations in Charleston Harbor and began to question "whether the creation of an Island on a shoal in the Channel, may not injuriously affect the navigation and commerce of the Harbor." The following month, the Committee on Federal Relations reported that it could not "ascertain by what authority the Government had assumed to erect the works alluded to." Acting apparently under the impression that a formal deed of cession to "land" ordinarily covered with water had not been necessary, the Federal Government had commenced operations at the mouth of Charleston Harbor without seeking or receiving State approval to do so.

Laval's claim was invalidated by the State's attorney general in 1837, but the harbor issue remained unresolved. It was November 1841 before the Federal Government received clear title to the 125 acres of harbor "land," although construction of Fort Sumter had resumed the previous January under the skillful guidance of Capt. A. H. Bowman, who pushed the work forward.

Bowman changed the original plans in several respects, the most important involving the composition of the foundation. Instead of a "grillage of continuous square timbers" upon the rock mass, he proposed laying several courses of granite blocks because he feared worms would completely destroy the wood; and palmetto, which might have resisted such attacks, did not have the compactness of fiber or the necessary strength to support the weight of the superstructure.

Work was difficult. The granite foundation had to be laid between periods of high and low tide, and there were times when the water level permitted no work to be done at all. The excessive heat of the Charleston summers was a recurrent problem; so was yellow fever. Much of the building material had to be brought in from the North. The magnitude of the task is indicated by the quantities involved: about 10,000 tons of granite (some of it from as far away as the Penobscot River region of Maine) and well over 60,000 tons of other rock. Bricks, shells, and sand could be obtained locally, but even here there were problems. Local brickyard capacities were small and millions of bricks were required. Similarly, hundreds of thousands of bushels of shells were needed—for concrete, for the foundation of the first-tier casemate floors, and for use in the parade fill next to the enrockment. Even the actual delivery of supplies, however local in origin, was a problem, for then, as now, the fort was a difficult spot at which to land.

By 1860 Fort Sumter outwardly possessed a commanding and formidable appearance. Its five-foot-thick pentagonal-shaped brick masonry walls towered nearly 50 feet above low water and enclosed a parade ground of roughly one acre. Along four of the walls extended two tiers of arched gunrooms. Officers' quarters lined the fifth side—the 316.7-foot gorge. (This wall was to be armed only along the parapet.) Three-story brick barracks for the enlisted garrison paralleled the gunrooms on each flank. The sally port at the center of the gorge opened on a 171-foot wharf and a 25½-foot-wide stone esplanade that

extended the length of that wall.

Outward appearances, however, were deceiving. Unruffled decades of peace had induced glacial slowness and indifference in Washington. The fort was far from completed and, according to U.S. Army Surgeon Samuel W. Crawford who came to know the place well, "in no condition for defense." Eight-foot-square openings yawned in place of gun embrasures on the second tier. Of the 135 guns planned for the gunrooms and the open terreplein above, only 15 had been mounted. Most of these were 32 pounders; none was heavier. The barracks were unfinished and, where tenable, occupied by workmen. The officers' quarters were also unfinished, and a large number of wooden structures "of the most temporary character" occupied the parade. These "served as storehouses for the tools and material of the workmen, while all over the parade lay sand and rough masonry, and sixty-six guns with their carriages and 5,600 shot and shell."

By December 1860 time as well as money had run out, and the fort was about to take on a political significance far beyond the military function it was originally intended to serve. The long-smoldering sectional dispute between North and South had become like a powder keg. And Fort Sumter was the fuse that would ignite it.

Part 2

CHARLESTON

MERCURY

EXTRA:

Passed unanimously at 1.15 o'clock, P. M. December 20th, 1860.

AN ORDINANCE

To dissolve the Union between the State of South Carolina and other States united with her under the compact entitled "The Constitution of the United States of America."

We, the People of the State of South Carolina, in Convention assembled, do declare and ordain, and it is hereby declared and ordained,

That the Ordinance adopted by us in Convention, on the twenty-third day of May, in the year of our Lord one thousand seven hundred and eighty-eight, whereby the Constitution of the United States of America was ratified, and also, all Acts and parts of Acts of the General Assembly of this State, ratifying amendments of the said Constitution, are hereby repealed; and that the union now subsisting between South Carolina and other States, under the name of "The United States of America," is hereby dissolved.

THE

UNION

IS

DISSOLVED!

Fort Sumter and the Coming of War, 1861

The headline in the Charleston *Mercury* summed it up aptly. After decades of sectional conflict, South Carolinians responded to the election of the first Republican President, Abraham Lincoln, by voting unanimously in convention on December 20, 1860, to secede from the Union. Within six weeks five other States—Mississippi, Florida, Alabama, Georgia, and Louisiana—followed her example. Early in February 1861 they met in Montgomery, Alabama, adopted a constitution, set up a provisional government—the Confederate States of America—and elected Jefferson Davis of Mississippi as President. By March 2, when Texas joined the Confederacy, nearly all the forts and naval yards in the seceded States had been seized by the new power. Fort Sumter was one of the handful that remained in Federal possession.

When South Carolina left the Union, the only post in Charleston Harbor garrisoned in strength by United States troops was Fort Moultrie on Sullivans Island. There, Maj. Robert Anderson commanded two companies of the First U.S. Artillery—about 85 officers and men. But six days after the secession ordinance was passed, Anderson, believing Moultrie to be indefensible, transferred his command to Fort Sumter. Unaware of an apparent pledge to maintain the harbor *status quo,* given by President James Buchanan some weeks before, Anderson acted in accordance with verbal instructions he received December 11 to *hold possession of the forts in this harbor, and if attacked . . . to defend yourself to the last extremity. The smallness of your force will not permit you, perhaps, to occupy more than one of the three forts, but an attack on or attempt to take possession of any of them will be regarded as an act of hostility, and you may then put your command into either of them which you may deem most proper to increase its power of resistance. You are also authorized to take similar steps whenever you have tangible evidence of a design to proceed to a hostile act.*

*President James Buchanan, who sought to maintain peace between the North and South during his final weeks in office. His uncharacteristically firm stand against South Carolina over the Sumter situation, however, risked the very conflict he sought to avoid. **Below:** Secretary of War John B. Floyd, onetime governor of Virginia and a strong secessionist sympathizer, condemned Anderson's occupation of Fort Sumter and urged President Buchanan not to send reinforcements.*

Anderson thought he had "tangible evidence" of hostile intent, both towards Fort Moultrie—an old fort vulnerable to land attack—and toward Fort Sumter, then occupied by about 80 engineer workmen. He moved, Anderson afterwards wrote to Secretary of War John B. Floyd, "to prevent the effusion of blood" and because he was certain "that if attacked my men must have been sacrificed, and the command of the harbor lost." To Anderson, a Kentuckian married to a Georgian, preservation of peace was of paramount importance. At the same time, as a veteran soldier of unquestioned loyalty, he had a duty to perform.

Charlestonians were outraged. Crowds collected in the streets; military organizations paraded; and "loud and violent were the expressions of feeling against Major Anderson and his action." On December 27 South Carolina volunteers occupied Fort Moultrie and Castle Pinckney, a third harbor fort, and began erecting defensive batteries elsewhere around the harbor. South Carolina's governor, Francis Pickens, regarded Anderson's move not only as an "outrageous breach of faith" but an act of aggression, and demanded, through commissioners sent to Washington, that the Federal Government evacuate Charleston Harbor. On December 28 President Buchanan, while admitting that the occupation of Sumter was against his policy, refused to accede to the demand.

The North was exultant. On New Year's Day, 1861, amid cheers for Major Anderson, salvos of artillery resounded in northern cities. By an imposing majority, the House of Representatives voted approval of Anderson's "bold and patriotic" act. The only question that remained was whether the national government would continue to support him.

At Fort Sumter, Anderson's 85 officers and men (plus the engineer workmen who remained after the fort was occupied) garrisoned a fortification intended for as many as 650 and had "about 4 months" supply of provisions. In January President Buchanan was persuaded to send off a relief expedition. Initial plans called for sending the sloop of war *Brooklyn* for this purpose, but when word arrived that the South Carolinians had obstructed the harbor entrance by sinking several ships, it was decided to use the *Star of the West,* an ordinary merchant ship, which would excite less suspicion and avoid the appearance of coercive intent. Two hundred men, small arms and ammunition, and several months' provisions were placed aboard. The men were to remain below deck on entering Charleston Harbor; the *Brooklyn* would follow, in case the *Star of the West* were fired upon and disabled.

But Charleston had been forewarned, and when the *Star of the West* appeared at the entrance of the harbor on January 9, 1861, cadets from the Citadel military college opened fire with several cannons mounted on Morris Island. The unarmed ship turned back. Anderson had held his fire, thinking the firing unauthorized. Orders authorizing supporting fire on his part had failed to reach him in time. For the moment, civil war had been avoided.

Further relief plans were now shelved, since President Buchanan was anxious to end his term of office in peace. Yet it was apparent that eventually the garrison would have to be supplied or the fort abandoned.

On January 10, Acting Secretary of War Joseph Holt (Floyd, a Southern sympathizer, had resigned over Buchanan's refusal to evacuate Fort Sumter) ordered Anderson to act strictly on the defensive. Anderson and Governor Pickens had already exchanged angry letters over the firing on the *Star of the West,* and when the major refused the governor's demand to surrender the fort (January 11), Pickens sent Isaac W. Haynes, the State's attorney general, to Washington to try once again to get the Federal troops removed. If this failed, Haynes was to offer to buy the fort from the government. President Buchanan refused to do either. The stalemate continued.

Fort Sumter was now preparing for attack. Thirty-eight more guns were mounted in the first tier of casemates and along the parapet, including heavier 42-pounders and Columbiads. Five Columbiads were mounted in the parade as mortars and three howitzers about the sally port (gateway) in the gorge. By April 12, a total of 60 guns were ready. "Bombproof" shelters and "splinter-proof" traverses were constructed on the parade ground and along the parapet. Overhanging galleries were built out from the parapet at strategic points for dropping shells on an assaulting force. Special protection was given the

*South Carolina's Governor Francis W. Pickens, who tried to persuade President Buchanan to order Anderson and his garrison back to Moultrie. "If I withdraw Anderson from Sumter," said the President, "I can travel home to Wheatland by the light of my own burning effigies." Anderson stayed and Pickens fumed. **Next pages:** One of several Columbiads that Anderson had mounted as mortars inside Fort Sumter to fire on Morris Island and Charleston. None of them, however, were used during the bombardment.*

President Abraham Lincoln wanted his inaugural address to convey a conciliatory message to the South. Most Southerners, however, like Emma Holmes of Charleston, thought it "stupid, ambiguous, vulgar and insolent" and "a virtual declaration of war." When Lincoln decided to send supplies to Anderson, Confederate efforts to force the evacuation of Sumter took on new urgency.

sally port. The second tier of casemates was left unarmed, however, and the 8-foot-square openings in the outer wall were bricked up. The small size of Anderson's garrison did not permit manning them.

Charleston, too, prepared. Besides continuing routine maintenance at Castle Pinckney and Fort Moultrie, additional batteries were set up on Sullivans Island, at Cummings Point on Morris Island, and outside Fort Johnson. An "ironclad" Columbiad battery, constructed of inclined logs plated with iron, was also mounted at Cummings Point. Meanwhile, Governor Pickens continued to allow Anderson to buy fresh meat and vegetables in town to supplement his garrison "issue" supply.

On March 1, the Confederate States government assumed control of military operations in and around Charleston Harbor and sent Brig. Gen. Pierre Gustave Toutant Beauregard to take command. Like Anderson, Beauregard (who arrived at Charleston on March 3) was a veteran of the Mexican War. He was a member of a Louisiana family of distinguished French lineage. Late captain in the U. S. Army, he had served briefly as superintendent of the U. S. Military Academy at West Point as recently as January. Once, years back, he had studied artillery there under Major Anderson. Now, pupil confronted master.

When Abraham Lincoln assumed office as President of the United States on March 4, he made it clear in a firm but generally conciliatory inaugural address that national authority must be upheld against the threat of disunion. As to the Federal forts and property in the seceded States, he said: "The power confided to me will be used to hold, occupy, and possess the property and places belonging to the Government. . . ." (He did not say "repossess.") Furthermore, there need be "no bloodshed or violence" as the result of this policy "unless it be forced upon the national authority." The President concluded:

In your hands, my dissatisfied fellow-countrymen, and not in mine, is the momentous issue of civil war. The Government will not assail you. You can have no conflict without being yourselves the aggressors. You have no oath registered in Heaven to destroy the Government, while I shall have the most solemn one to 'preserve, protect, and defend' it.

The Sumter situation was placed squarely before Lincoln on the day he assumed office. On the morning of Inaugural Day outgoing Secretary of War Holt received a dispatch from Major Anderson indicating that the remainder of the "issue" rations brought over from Fort Moultrie in December would last only a few more weeks. He might be able to hold out longer if he was able to maintain his local fresh food supply, but if that were cut off, the garrison would be in desperate straits. As to reenforcements, given the state of local Confederate preparations, an estimated force of 20,000 men would now be needed to return Federal authority to Charleston Harbor. Given these circumstances, reenforcement was out of the question. The entire Army of the United States numbered less than 16,000 men. "Evacuation seems almost inevitable," wrote General in Chief Winfield Scott; the majority of Lincoln's Cabinet agreed. The President, however, was not yet willing to concede that point and sent Capt. Gustavus W. Fox, onetime U.S. Navy officer and long an advocate of a relief expedition, to Charleston to talk directly with Anderson. In the meantime, reassured by Secretary of State William Seward and others, the South came to believe that Fort Sumter would be evacuated.

On April 4, Lincoln's Secretary of War, Simon Cameron, informed Major Anderson that an attempt would be made to supply him with provisions "and, in case the effort is resisted . . . to reenforce you." Convinced from Captain Fox's on-the-spot reports that such an expedition was feasible, and that there was no Union sentiment in South Carolina to which to appeal, Lincoln had decided on the nearest thing to preserving the *status quo.* Merchant steamers under cover of ships of war would carry "subsistence and other supplies" to Anderson; the warships (with troop reinforcements on board) would be used only if a peaceable landing were opposed. Fox would command. Meanwhile, in accordance with a pledge already given, the governor of South Carolina would be carefully informed in advance.

The announcement of the expedition to supply Fort Sumter was the spark that set off the explosive forces which had been building up since 1850. The Confederate capital at Montgomery was informed. Anderson's supply of fresh provisions had already been cut off on the 7th; now, his mail was seized.

Work was pushed on the harbor fortifications. A new battery mounting two 24-pounders and two 32-

Confederate President Jefferson Davis likewise sought to temper the growing sectional dispute, and sent commissioners to Washington to try to settle "all questions of disagreement between the two governments." When the commissioners informed him that the Lincoln government "declines to recognize our official character or the power we represent," Davis ordered Beauregard to demand Sumter's surrender— "and if this is refused proceed . . . to reduce it."

pounders was unmasked on Sullivans Island; another ironclad battery was put into position at its western tip. Originally designed to be "floating," this battery mounted two heavy 42-pounders in addition to two 32-pounders. Near Mount Pleasant another (10-inch) mortar battery was installed. At Fort Moultrie, 11 guns now bore on Fort Sumter, including three 8-inch Columbiads. Additional guns were mounted to command the harbor channels and to guard against landings by the Federal fleet. Three thousand more Confederate troops were called, bringing the number already on the post to 3,700. The harbor seethed with activity.

"The gage is thrown down," said the Charleston *Mercury*, "and we accept the challenge. We will meet the invader, and God and Battle must decide the issue between the hirelings of Abolition hate and Northern tyranny, and the people of South Carolina defending their freedom and their homes." A small 12-pounder Blakely rifled cannon arrived from England—a gift of a Charlestonian residing in London. Mounted at Cummings Point, it proved an ominous forerunner of the powerful rifled guns that two years later would reduce Fort Sumter to rubble.

After cabinet debate in Montgomery, the Confederate Secretary of War, Leroy Pope Walker, ordered General Beauregard to demand the evacuation of the fort, and if that demand was refused, to "reduce it." On the afternoon of April 11, three of Beauregard's aides visited the fort under a flag of truce and presented the ultimatum. Major Anderson refused compliance but at the same time said, "Gentlemen, if you do not batter the fort to pieces about us, we shall be starved out in a few days." Still reluctant to initiate conflict, the Montgomery government telegraphed Beauregard: *Do not desire needlessly to bombard Fort Sumter. If Major Anderson will state the time at which . . . he will evacuate, and agree that in the meantime he will not use his guns against us unless ours should be employed against Fort Sumter, you are authorized thus to avoid the effusion of blood. If this or its equivalent be refused, reduce the fort. . . .*

The atmosphere in Charleston was tense. In at least one household, dinner was the "merriest, maddest . . . yet. Men were more audaciously wise and witty. We had an unspoken foreboding it was to be our last pleasant meeting."

Gen. P.G.T. Beauregard told Confederate Secretary of War Leroy Pope Walker that "if Sumter was properly garrisoned and armed, it would be a perfect Gibralter to anything but constant shelling, night and day, from the four points of the compass. As it is, the weakness of the garrison constitutes our greatest advantage, and we must, for the present, turn our attention to preventing it from being re-enforced . . . but, should we have to open our batteries upon it, I hope to be able to do so with all the advantage the condition of things here will permit." The map at right, taken from Harper's Weekly, *shows Fort Sumter and the Confederate batteries erected against it in 1861. Beauregard's view of Sumter as a Gibralter was confirmed during the 1863-65 siege of Charleston.*

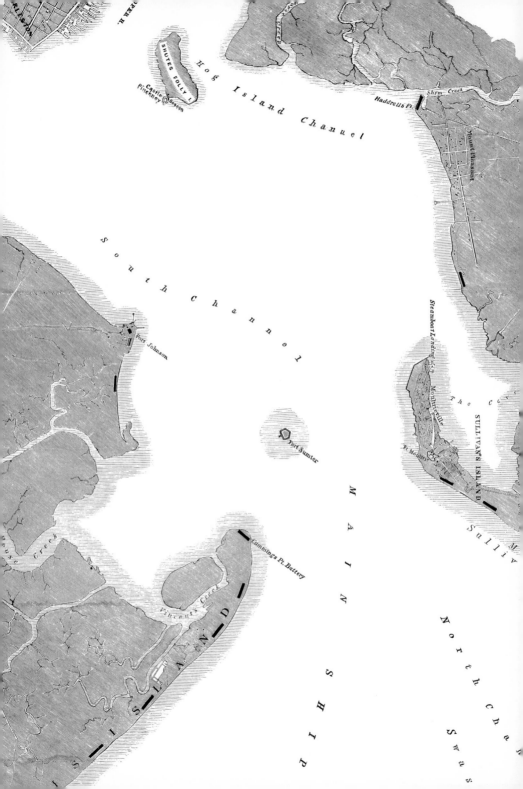

Among the members of Beauregard's staff who took part in the negotiations with Major Anderson prior to the bombardment of Fort Sumter were two South Carolinians—Capt. Stephen D. Lee (above), a 28-year-old West Point graduate and an officer in the South Carolina volunteers, and Col. James Chesnut (below), 46-year-old former U.S. Senator but now a member of the Confederate Congress.

Shortly after midnight, four Confederate officers confronted Anderson again. About three hours later, in a carefully worded reply, the Union commander agreed to evacuate "by noon on the 15th" unless he should receive prior to that time "controlling instructions from my Government or additional supplies." But it was expected in Charleston that the Federal supply ships would arrive before the 15th. Anderson's reply was rejected by the Confederate officers, who proceeded at once to Fort Johnson to give the order to open fire.

At 4:30 a.m., a mortar shell from Fort Johnson arched across the sky and burst almost directly over Fort Sumter. This was the signal for opening the bombardment. Within a few minutes, a ring of cannons and mortars about the harbor—43 in all—were firing at Sumter. Major Anderson withheld fire until about 7 o'clock. Then Capt. Abner Doubleday, Anderson's second in command, fired a shot at the ironclad battery on Cummings Point. Ominously, the light shot "bounded off from the sloping roof . . . without producing any apparent effect." Not at any time during the battle did the guns of Fort Sumter do great damage to the Confederate defenses. Most of Fort Sumter's heaviest guns were on the parapet and in the parade. To reduce casualties in the small garrison, Anderson ordered these left unmanned. For a while, with the help of the engineer workmen remaining at the fort, nine or ten of the casemate guns were manned. But by noon, the expenditure of ammunition was so rapid that the firing was restricted to six guns only. Meanwhile, an eyewitness later recorded, *Showers of balls from 10-inch Columbiads and 42 pounders, and shells from [10-] inch mortars poured into the fort in one incessant stream, causing great flakes of masonry to fall in all directions. When the immense mortar shells, after sailing high in the air, came down in a vertical direction, and buried themselves in the parade ground, their explosion shook the fort like an earthquake.*

All Charleston watched. Business was entirely suspended. King Street was deserted. The Battery, the wharves and shipping, and "every steeple and cupola in the city" were crowded with anxious spectators. And "never before had such crowds of ladies without attendants" visited the streets of Charleston. "The women were wild" on the housetops. In the darkness before dawn there were "Prayers from the women and imprecations from the men; and then a shell would light up the scene." As the day advanced, the city became rife with rumors: "Tonight, they say, the forces are to attempt to land. The *Harriet Lane* had her wheel house smashed and put back to sea. . . . We hear nothing, can listen to nothing. Boom boom goes the cannon all the time. The nervous strain is awful. . . ." Volunteers rushed to join their companies. There was "Stark Means marching under the piazza at the head of his regiment . . .," his proud mother leaning over the balcony rail "looking with tearful eyes." Two members of the Palmetto Guard paid $50 for a boat to carry them to Morris Island.

The barracks at Fort Sumter caught fire three times that first day, but each time the fire was extinguished. One gun on the parapet was dismounted; another was damaged. The wall about one embrasure was shattered to a depth of 20 inches. That was caused, in part, by the Blakely rifle, firing with "the accuracy of a duelling pistol." The quarters on the gorge were completely riddled. When night came, dark and stormy, Fort Sumter's fire ceased entirely. Using the six needles available, the work of making cartridge bags continued; blankets, old clothing, extra hospital sheets, and even paper, were used in the emergency. Meantime, the supply fleet, off the bar since the onset of hostilities, did no more than maintain its position. It had been crippled upon departure when Seward's meddling caused withdrawal of the powerful warship *Powhatan*. Now, bad weather prevented even a minimum supporting operation.

On the morning of the 13th, Sumter opened "early and spitefully," and, with the increased supply of cartridges, kept up a brisk fire for a while. About mid-morning "hotshot" (solid cannonballs heated red hot) set fire to the officers' quarters. The Confederate fire then increased; soon the whole extent of the quarters was in flames, endangering the powder magazines. The blaze spread to the barracks. By noon the fort was almost uninhabitable. The men crowded to the embrasures for air or lay on the ground with handkerchiefs over their mouths. Valiant efforts by Anderson's men had saved some of the powder before the onrush of the flames forced the closing of the magazines, and the fort's defenders continued to fire. At every shot, Beauregard later reported, the

Ardent Virginia secessionist Edmund Ruffin (above) has long been credited by some historians with firing the first shot against Fort Sumter. The honor actually belongs to Capt. George S. James, commander of the 10-inch mortar batteries on James Island, who ordered the signal shell fired from Fort Johnson. Ruffin, however, did fire the first shot from the Ironclad Battery on Cummings Point. Below: Capt. (later Gen.) Abner Doubleday, who directed the first return shot from Fort Sumter.

Confederate troops, "carried away by their natural generous impulses, mounted the different batteries, and . . . cheered the garrison for its pluck and gallantry and hooted the fleet lying inactive just outside the bar."

About 1:30 in the afternoon the flag was shot down. Almost accidentally, this led to surrender. By authority of Gen. James Simons, commanding on Morris Island, Col. Louis T. Wigfall, a former Texas senator and now one of Beauregard's aides detached for duty at that spot, set out by small boat to ascertain whether Anderson would capitulate. Before he arrived at the beleagured fort, the United States flag was again flying, but Wigfall rowed on. The firing continued from the batteries across the harbor. Attaching a white handkerchief to the point of his sword, Wigfall entered the fort through an embrasure on the left flank and offered the Federal commander any terms he desired, the precise nature of which would have to be arranged with General Beauregard. Anderson accepted on the basis of Beauregard's original terms: evacuation with his command, taking arms and all private and company property, saluting the United States flag as it was lowered, and being conveyed, if desired, to a Northern port. The white flag went up again; the firing ceased. Wigfall departed confident that Anderson had surrendered unconditionally. He and his boatman were borne ashore in triumph.

Meanwhile, officers had arrived at the fort from General Beauregard's headquarters in Charleston. From these men, dispatched to offer assistance to the Federal commander, Anderson learned that Wigfall's action was unauthorized; that, indeed, the colonel had not seen the commanding general since the start of the battle. From another party of officers he learned Beauregard's exact terms of surrender. They failed to include the privilege of saluting the flag, though in all other respects they were the same as those Anderson had believed he had accepted from Wigfall. Impetuously, Anderson had first declared he would run up his flag again. Then, restrained by Beauregard's aides, he waited while his request for permission to salute the flag was conveyed to the commanding general. In the course of the afternoon, Beauregard courteously sent over a fire engine from the city. About 7:30 that evening,

*Louis T. Wigfall, the Yankee-hating former U.S. Senator from Texas, who unofficially negotiated and received Anderson's surrender of Fort Sumter. **Opposite:** Charlestonians—men, women, and children—watch from the rooftops as Confederate batteries bombard Sumter. Anderson's delay in returning the fire caused many to believe that he did not intend to respond at all—a situation which, in Edmund Ruffin's view, "would have cheapened our conquest."*

The Fort Sumter Flags

When Maj. Robert Anderson transferred his small Federal garrison from Fort Moultrie to Fort Sumter on the night of December 26, 1860, he took with him not only needed supplies and equipment but the two flags of his command—the 20-by-36-foot garrison flag, which he carried himself, and the smaller storm flag used during bad weather. At noon on December 27, following a prayer of thanksgiving for their safe arrival (shown in the painting on these pages), the garrison flag was raised above Sumter.

2

3

The garrison flag (the remnants of which are shown in photograph no. 1 at left) continued to mark Anderson's occupation of the fort until April 11, 1861, when, having become torn, it was replaced by the 10-foot by 20-foot storm flag (no. 2) which flew during the subsequent two-day bombardment.

After the fort's surrender on April 14, Anderson took both flags with him to New York City. There, following their display in a massive patriotic demonstration in Union Square, they were boxed up and placed in storage. The flags remained with the Anderson family until 1905, when they were presented to then Secretary of War William Howard Taft. The War Department transferred them to the National Park Service in 1954. They are now part of the collections of Fort Sumter National Monument. A third flag in the park's collection is the 6-foot by 9-foot flag of the Palmetto Guards (no. 3), which was the first Southern banner to be raised over Sumter's walls after Anderson's evacuation.

Beauregard's chief of staff returned with word that Anderson's request would be granted and the terms offered on the 11th would be faithfully adhered to. The engagement was officially at an end. During the 34-hour bombardment, more than 3,000 shells had been hurled at the fort.

On Sunday, April 14, Anderson and his garrison marched out of the fort with drums beating and colors flying and boarded the steamer *Isabel* to join the Federal fleet off the bar. The only fatality of the engagement occurred just prior to leaving when, on the 47th round of what was to have been a 100-gun salute to the United States flag, one of the guns discharged prematurely, exploding a pile of cartridges and causing the death of Pvt. Daniel Hough. Another man, Pvt. Edward Galloway, was mortally wounded and died several days later. The 50th round was the last. Now, as the *Isabel* carrying Anderson's command steamed down the channel, the soldiers at the Confederate battery on Cummings Point lined the beach, heads uncovered, in silent tribute to Sumter's defenders.

The following day, April 15, 1861, President Lincoln issued a call for 75,000 militia. Soon the States of Virginia, Arkansas, Tennessee, and North Carolina joined the Confederacy. Civil war, so long dreaded, had begun.

The Struggle for Charleston, 1863-65

With Fort Sumter in Confederate hands, the port of Charleston became an irritating loophole in the Federal naval blockade of the Atlantic coast—doubly so because at Charleston "rebellion first lighted the flame of civil war." As late as January 1863, vessels plied to and from Charleston and the Bahamas "with the certainty and promptness of a regular line," bringing needed war supplies in exchange for cotton.

Capture of Port Royal Harbor on November 7, 1861, by a Federal fleet under Capt. Samuel F. Du Pont, however, had made possible land and sea operations against Charleston. In June 1862, an attempt was made by Federal Maj. Gen. David Hunter to push through to the city by James Island on the south. This ended in Union disaster at the bloody battle of Secessionville. Meanwhile, the *Monitor-Virginia (Merrimack)* action in Hampton Roads had demonstrated the feasibility of an "ironclad" naval expedition against Fort Sumter, the key to the harbor. Sumter, rebuilt and strengthened, was now a formidable work armed with some 95 guns and garrisoned with upwards of 500 men. By May 1862, the Navy Department seemed possessed of what then Rear Admiral Du Pont was calling a "morbid appetite" to capture Charleston. But the War Department, far from supplying the additional troops to Hunter's command, withdrew units to reenforce Gen. George B. McClellan's army in its campaign against Richmond, the Confederate capital.

On April 5, 1863, a fleet of nine Federal ironclads, armed with 32 heavy-caliber guns, appeared off Charleston bar. Seven were of the single-turret "cheesebox on a raft" *Monitor*-type; one, the *Keokuk,* was a double-turreted affair; and the last, the flagship *New Ironsides,* was an ironclad frigate. With ebb tide on the afternoon of the 7th, the "new-fangled" ironclads steamed single-file up the main ship channel east of Morris Island. The weather was clear and bright; the water "as stable as of a

river." By 3 o'clock, the *Weehawken,* the leading monitor, had come within range, and Fort Moultrie opened fire. The *Passaic,* second in line, responded. Fort Sumter held fire, its guns trained on a buoy at the turn of the channel. When the *Weehawken* came abreast of that point, Sumter's right flank guns let loose. These were followed by all the guns on Sullivans Island, at Fort Moultrie, and at Cummings Point that could be brought to bear.

It was too much for the slow and unwieldy ironclads. In the course of the 2½-hour fight, only one came within 900 yards of Fort Sumter. To the 2,209 rounds hurled against them, the ironclads were able to return 154, only 34 of which found the target. These breached and loosened 25 feet of the right flank parapet and pocked the walls elsewhere with craters up to 2½ feet deep. But it was far from enough; Fort Sumter remained strong and secure. On the other hand, five of the ironclads were seriously disabled by the accurate Confederate fire, and one, the *Keokuk,* sank the following morning in the shallow water off Morris Island. Confederate troops later recovered the guns of the *Keokuk* and mounted one of them at Fort Sumter.

The North, confident of victory, was stunned by Du Pont's failure at a time when the general military situation was gloomy. The war in the East had been bloody and indecisive; the news from the West was no better. Federal authorities now looked to a combined operation to seize Morris Island and from there demolish Fort Sumter. With Fort Sumter reduced, the harbor could be entered.

Folly Island and Coles Island, next south of Morris Island, had been occupied by Northern troops just prior to the naval attack. In June and July, the north end of Folly Island was fortified. In a remarkable operation, 47 guns and mortars were secretly emplaced "within speaking distance of the enemy's pickets." Some 11,000 men were concentrated on the island. Brig. Gen. Quincy A. Gillmore, the "breacher" of Fort Pulaski, took command on June 12. Rear Adm. John A. Dahlgren superseded Admiral Du Pont on July 6.

During that time the Confederates mounted guns at the south end of Morris Island and strengthened the earthworks at its upper end—Battery Gregg at Cummings Point and Battery Wagner some 1,400

Rear Adm. Samuel F. Du Pont, commander of the South Atlantic Blockading Squadron. The repulse of the navy's April 7, 1863, attempt to capture Charleston (depicted at left in a contemporary engraving from Harper's Weekly) *persuaded Du Pont "that the place cannot be taken by a purely naval attack." The admiral's pessimism about ironclad ships of war and his decision not to renew the attack on Charleston angered the Navy Department and led to his removal from command.*

Maj. Gen. Quincy A. Gill-more, commander of the Federal land forces besieging Charleston, 1863-64. In the year that he spent at Charleston, Gillmore and Du Pont's replacement, Rear Adm. John A. Dahlgren (below), conducted a cooperative and sustained operation that resulted in the capture of Morris Island and Battery Wagner and the virtual demolition of Fort Sumter. Right: Part of Gillmore's map of the Charleston defenses.

yards to the south. The latter work, commanding the island at its narrowest point, was made into a formidable "sand fort" mounting about 15 guns.

Fort Sumter, 1,390 yards distant from Battery Gregg, prepared for siege, too. Brick and stone masonry "counter-forts," already built at each extremity of the esplanade as protection for the magazines, were now strengthened, and much of the remaining gorge exterior was sandbagged or otherwise protected. The casemates on the right or sea front flank were filled with sand, and the rooms on the gorge were filled with damp cotton bales laid in sand. The upper-tier magazines were abandoned and filled with sandbags to protect the magazines below. Protective revetments and other defensive devices were introduced at various points throughout the fort. Frequently during this period the garrison was host to officers on leave, citizens of Charleston, and even many ladies, who came to see the scars of the April battle, to admire the drill, or to observe the preparations. At the end of June 1863, Fort Sumter was garrisoned by five companies (perhaps 500 men) of the First South Carolina Artillery, under command of Col. Alfred Rhett. Its armament had been reduced to 68 guns and mortars, many of the best pieces having been removed to strengthen other fortifications about the harbor.

On the morning of July 10, 3,000 Union infantry, supported by four monitors and the artillery on Folly Island, descended on the southern end of Morris Island. Directing the attack was Brig. Gen. Truman Seymour, a company commander at Fort Sumter two years before. Within four hours, most of the Island was in his hands. The Confederate forces, outgunned and outmanned, fell back to Battery Wagner. Sumter's guns helped to cover their retreat.

A "desperate" assault upon Wagner the next morning failed, though the parapet was briefly gained. General Gillmore established counter-batteries and tried again on the 18th. From noon until nightfall that day, "without cessation or intermission," Federal guns poured a "storm of shot and shell upon Fort Wagner . . . perhaps unequalled in history." This was followed by an attack by some 6,000 troops, spearheaded by the 54th Massachusetts, the first U.S. black regiment to go to war. In a short, savage struggle, Seymour's force suffered 1,500 cas-

Col. Alfred Rhett (above) commanded Fort Sumter during the April 1863 ironclad attack and the first great bombardment of August-September. Below: Brig. Gen. Truman Seymour, who served at Fort Sumter under Anderson in 1860-61, commanded the assault troops that captured Morris Island in July 1863. He was severely wounded in the subsequent attack on Battery Wagner.

ualties. Though one angle of the fort was gained and held for a time, the attack was repulsed.

Thwarted in his plan to secure easy possession of Morris Island as a base for breaching operations against Fort Sumter, Gillmore now determined to batter the fort into submission from the ground he already possessed. Batteries Wagner and Gregg would be taken by protracted siege operations. Anticipating that Sumter was "liable to be silenced sooner or later" and fearing attack at other points about the harbor, Confederate authorities continued to remove the fort's guns and ammunition for use elsewhere. By mid-August, Sumter's armament was reduced to 38 cannon and two mortars.

At distances of 2 to 2½ miles from Fort Sumter—distances extraordinary for such operations—Gillmore set up eight batteries of heavy rifled cannon. In the marsh west of Morris Island, where the mud was like liquid, his engineers successfully placed a 200-pounder Parrott rifle—the notorious "Swamp Angel"—to fire on Charleston.

Gillmore's batteries did some experimental firing in late July and early August, testing the range and the effects of their shots on Sumter. The real bombardment began on August 17, with nearly 1,000 shells being fired that first day alone. Almost 5,000 more were fired during the week that followed. Even at the end of the first day it was obvious that the fort was never intended to withstand the heavy Parrotts. Three days later, a monstrous 13-ton Parrott rifle hurling 250-pound shells was added to Gillmore's armament, making 18 rifled cannon in action. The range kept Sumter from replying to the land batteries, and the monitors appeared only fleetingly.

On the 21st, with the "Swamp Angel" in position, Gillmore demanded the evacuation of Fort Sumter and Morris Island. Otherwise he would fire on Charleston. The ultimatum was unsigned, however, and before the Confederates could confirm its origin, Gillmore had opened fire. But little damage had been done when, on the 36th round, the "Swamp Angel" burst. Meanwhile, Beauregard had delivered an indignant reply. The bombardment of Sumter continued.

Early on the 23d, against Dahlgren's ironclads, Fort Sumter fired what proved to be its last shots in action. Its brick masonry walls were shattered and undermined; a breach 8 by 10 feet yawned in the upper casemates of the left face; at points, the sloped debris of the walls already provided a practicable route for assault. Still, the Confederate garrison, supplemented by a force of 200 to 400 blacks, labored night and day, strengthening and repairing the defenses. The debris, accumulating above the sand- and cotton-filled rooms, itself bolstered the crumbling walls. By the 24th, Gillmore was able to report the "practical demolition" of the fort. On the 26th General Beauregard ordered the fort held "to the last extremity."

The bombardment continued sporadically during the following week. On the night of September 1-2, the ironclads moved against the fort—the first major naval operation against Fort Sumter since the preceding April. For five hours, the frigate *New Ironsides* and five monitors bombarded the fort, now without a gun with which to answer the "sneaking sea-devils." Two hundred and forty-five shot and shell were hurled against the ruins—twice as many as were thrown in the April attack. The tidal conditions, plus a "rapid and sustained" fire from Fort Moultrie, forced the monitors to withdraw.

Some desultory firing on the 2d brought to an end the first sustained bombardment of Fort Sumter. More than 7,300 rounds had been hurled against the fort since August 17. Now, with the fort reduced to a "shapeless and harmless mass of ruins," the Federals could concentrate on Battery Wagner, only 100 yards from Gillmore's forward trenches.

On the morning of September 5, Federal cannoneers began a devastating barrage against Battery Wagner. For 42 hours, night and day, in what General Gillmore called a spectacle "of surpassing sublimity and grandeur," 17 mortars and nine rifled cannon, as well as the powerful guns of the ironclads, pounded the earthwork. Calcium lights turned night into day. On the night of September 6-7, the Confederates evacuated Wagner and Gregg. Morris Island was at last in Union hands.

Fort Sumter, however, remained defiant. When Dahlgren demanded the fort's surrender, on the morning of the 7th, General Beauregard sent word that the admiral could have it when he could "take it and hold it." On September 4 the garrison had been relieved by fresh troops, 320 strong. Maj. Stephen Elliott succeeded to the command.

The Fight for Battery Wagner

On July 10, 1863, Union forces successfully invaded Morris Island, a narrow stretch of land which formed the southern entrance to Charleston Harbor. The Confederate defenders were pushed back nearly 3 miles to a strong fortification known as Battery Wagner, whose heavy guns commanded nearly the entire length of the island. Gen. Quincy A. Gillmore knew that this fort would have to be taken if Morris Island was to serve as a base of operations against Charleston.

Accordingly, at dusk on July 18th, three Union brigades numbering about 6,000 men commanded by Gen. Truman Seymour assembled for an assault on Battery Wagner. Assigned to lead the column was Col. Robert Gould Shaw's 54th Massachusetts Infantry, composed of 600 free-black men recruited from various Northern States. "We shall take the fort or die there!" shouted Colonel Shaw

(right) as Seymour ordered the troops forward.

Wagner's artillery opened fire when the Federals were within 200 yards of the battery. Then the fort's defenders, North and South Carolina troops, let fly a volley of musketry that tore huge gaps in the Union ranks. Those who survived this terrible fire, having reached the ditch in front of the fort, sloshed through 3 feet of water and scrambled up the walls of the parapet bravely waving both the national flag and the Massachusetts State colors.

Shaw himself gained the rampart and shouted, "Forward, Fifty-fourth!", then fell dead with a bullet in his heart.

Now other Federal regiments joined in the attack, but after several hours of desperate fighting, including hand-to-hand combat on Wagner's parapet, the Feder-als were driven back. Bodies lay piled three deep in front of the fort and 9 of the 10 Union regimental commanders were killed or wounded. The 54th Massachusetts alone lost nearly 40 percent of the men engaged.

Battery Wagner finally came into Union hands on September 6, 1863, after the Confederates were ordered to evacuate Morris Island entirely. Contrary to Northern expectations, Fort Sumter and the city of Charleston did not fall into Federal possession until February 1865.

Maj. Stephen Elliott, one-time captain of the Beaufort (Light) Artillery, assumed command of the Fort Sumter ruins in September 1863 at the personal request of General Beauregard. Elliott remained in charge until May 1864, when he was transferred to command a regiment in Virginia.

Dahlgren "immediately designed to put into operation a plan to capture Fort Sumter." Accordingly the monitor *Weehawken* was ordered "to cut off all communication" via Cummings Point, while *New Ironsides* and the remaining ironclads moved up "to feel, and if possible, pass" the obstructions thought to be in the channel north of the fort. But *Weehawken* grounded, and the monitors caught such a severe fire from Fort Moultrie and the other Confederate batteries on Sullivans Island, that the admiral "deemed it best to give [his] entire attention to the *Weehawken*" and withdraw. Whatever his original plan, Dahlgren now decided upon a small-boat assault. The task seemed simple: with "nothing but a corporal's guard in the fort," all he had to do was "go and take possession."

On the night of September 8-9, 400 sailors and marines made the attempt. A tug towed the small boats within 800 yards of the fort, then cast them loose. In the darkness and confusion, plans went awry and two columns advanced simultaneously upon the right flank of the fort. The Confederates coolly held their fire till the Federals in the lead boats began to land, then let loose with musketry, hand grenades, "fire balls," grape and canister, brickbats, and masonry fragments. At a signal from the fort, the Confederate gunboat *Chicora* steamed out from the harbor and opened fire; Fort Moultrie "fired like a devil."

From the outer boats, the marines replied rapidly for a few minutes. Some of the sailors ashore fired a few shots from their revolvers, but most sought refuge in the embrasures or breaches in the wall. It was all over in 20 minutes. Most of the boats did not even touch shore. The Federal loss was 124 killed, wounded, and captured, and five boats were taken. A similar expedition from Gillmore's command was detained by low tide in a creek west of Morris Island. Service rivalry had prevented active cooperation that might have resulted in victory.

Except for a six-day bombardment of "minor" proportions late in September, Fort Sumter was free of attack for almost two months. Damages sustained by the monitors in the Morris Island operation, as much as Fort Moultrie's increased firepower and the fear of channel obstructions (a menace which later proved to be greatly exaggerated), made Admiral

Dahlgren reluctant to make another move at this time. General Gillmore, engaged now in rebuilding and rearming the captured Confederate batteries on Cummings Point, thought he had accomplished his part of the operation. In his opinion, Fort Sumter was effectively reduced; its actual seizure and occupation would be costly and unnecessary; besides, the reinforcements needed for such an undertaking were not available anyway. Indeed, with the Confederate surrender of Vicksburg and the defeat of Gen. Robert E. Lee's army at Gettysburg, Charleston had suddenly become much less important. Gillmore contemplated no further offensive operations by his forces.

On October 26, having learned that the Confederates were remounting some of Sumter's guns, Gillmore resumed the bombardment. For the next 12 days, the concentration of fire was comparable to the great bombardment of the preceding August. But now, with the new batteries on Cummings Point in operation and the range shortened to less than a mile, the effect was far greater. For the first time, 16 heavy mortars were in use—two of them 8½-ton pieces (13-inch bore) throwing 200-pound projectiles. Their sharp, plunging fire was added to that of 12 Parrott rifles—the types already used so effectively against the fort—and one powerful Columbiad. In addition, two monitors, with guns "equal to a dozen" Parrotts, crossed fire with Gillmore's artillery.

Sumter's sea front (right flank), upright and relatively unscathed till now, was breached for nearly half its length. The ramparts and arches of its upper casemates were cut down and the interior barracks demolished. The accumulated debris made ascent easy inside and out. Through the breach, the Federal guns took the channel fronts in reverse. Exposed to direct fire for the first time, they were soon cut and jagged. Still, the gorge ruin remained much the same; to Admiral Dahlgren, that "heap of rubbish" looked invincible.

Night and day throughout November and into December, Gillmore's batteries, assisted occasionally by the monitors, maintained a slow fire against the fort. Sumter could respond with merely "harmless musketry," but its defenders seemed "snug in the ruins." And if Sumter was without cannons, Confederate batteries on James and Sullivans Islands kept up an irritating counterfire.

Sumter Under Fire

By August 23, 1863, when the photograph at right was taken from the northern tip of Morris Island, General Gillmore's siege guns had been firing at Fort Sumter continuously for a week in what came to be known as the "First Great Bombardment." By then, according to Gen. J. W. Turner, Gillmore's chief of artillery, "The demolition of the fort . . . was complete so far as its offensive powers were considered. Every gun upon the parapet was either dismounted or seriously damaged. The parapet could be

seen in many places both on the sea and channel faces to be completely torn away from the *terre-plein*. The place, in fine, was a ruin, and effectually disabled for any immediate defense of the harbor of Charleston."

General Turner's assessment of Fort Sumter's "demolition" proved premature. Thanks to the efforts of its garrison over the next several months, the fort was transformed, according to chief engineer Maj. John Johnson, from "a shapeless pile of shattered walls and casemates, showing here and there the guns disabled and half buried in splintered wrecks of carriages, its mounds of rubbish fairly reeking with the smoke and smell of powder, . . . into a powerful earthwork, impregnable to assault, and even supporting the other works at the entrance of Charleston harbor with six guns of the heaviest caliber."

The damage caused to the fort's interior during Gillmore's "First Great Bombardment" is evident in the remarkable "action" photograph below, taken by Charleston photographer George S. Cook on September 8, 1863, just as a shell from the Federal ironclad *Weehawken* burst on the rubble-strewn parade ground during Admiral Dahlgren's naval assault on the harbor batteries.

Maj. John A. Johnson, commanding engineer at Fort Sumter during the 1863-65 Confederate occupation.

On November 6, the Confederate engineer at Fort Sumter, Maj. John Johnson, reported that while the height of the mass of the fort was "diminishing visibly on the sides away from the city, when it gets down to the lower casemates it will have become so thick from accumulated debris as to resist further battering." Two weeks later, he found the fort stronger than ever, with casualties surprisingly low — only two men were killed in the August bombardment and only 22 more since the start of the present one; 118 had been wounded. Johnson was not fearful of being driven out by the big Federal guns, but rather "exposure to assault from barges at night."

In mid-November such an attack seemed to be forthcoming. During the early hours of the 18th, the defenders of the fort had four distinct alarms as small boats approached within hailing distance; "all hands out each time and expecting a fight." On the following night, a force estimated at 250 men approached within 300 yards of the fort, only to be driven off by the muskets of the aroused garrison. This was not, however, a real attack but only a reconnaissance ordered by Gillmore "with a view to compel the garrison to show its strength." Having done that, he would now wait for the Navy to make the next move.

But Admiral Dahlgren could not move until the repairs on the monitors were finished, and as late as January 1864 these still were not completed. Even so, confronted with reports of greatly strengthened harbor fortifications and a growing concern over the exact nature of the harbor obstructions, he was reluctant to move without additional monitors. Defeat was always possible, and defeat for the Union's only ironclad squadron might have serious consequences — not only for the blockade and Gillmore's command on Morris Island, but for operations elsewhere along the coast. Nevertheless, substantial advantages had already been gained: the blockade at Charleston was tighter with Morris Island in Federal hands. To all this, the Navy Department agreed. Elsewhere, while Dahlgren and Gillmore marked time, the war gathered momentum. In November 1863, the North won decisively at Chattanooga.

The additional monitors, always promised, never seemed to arrive. On December 5, General Gillmore stopped the bombardment of Fort Sumter begun 41 days earlier. There seemed no great advantage in continuing, and it required considerable ammunition. He had made his last sustained effort against the fort. On only four other days in December did he fire any rounds at all. During the four months he remained in command, the firing was intermittent, never more than "minor" in character. Meanwhile, Gen. Ulysses S. Grant's forthcoming operations in Virginia required all available troops. On May 1, 1864, Gillmore departed for Fort Monroe with 18,000 picked men and quantities of valuable matériel.

Dahlgren's much-needed monitors never did arrive (Grant needed those, too) and, with the monitor force he did have reduced to six by the foundering of the *Weehawken* in December, further offensive operations against Charleston seemed completely out of the question. In June, the ironclad frigate *New Ironsides* was withdrawn to the north.

In the preceding December, Fort Sumter had been an almost chaotic ruin. But with the fort practically left alone during the months immediately following, the garrison gradually restored order from chaos. The parade ground, excavated well below high-water level to provide sand-filling, was cleared, drained, and partially rebuilt. Trim ranks of gabions (wicker baskets filled with sand) bolstered the sloping debris of the walls on the interior. The three-gun battery in the lower right face was lined with logs and planks, 10 feet deep, and revetted more thoroughly in the rear. In casemates on the left flank another three-gun battery was created. Through the disordered debris of the left and right faces, the garrison tunneled a 275-foot timbered gallery connecting the two batteries and fort headquarters in the left flank. And in from the rubble of the sea front, the garrison built a loopholed timber blockhouse to cover the parade ground in the event of further assault. In May, Capt. John C. Mitchel, son of the Irish patriot, relieved Lt. Col. Stephen Elliott in command.

The onset of summer, 1864, brought one more attempt to take Fort Sumter; likewise another officer of the original Fort Sumter garrison came into the operation. Maj. Gen. John G. Foster, engineer of the fort in April 1861, had succeeded to Gillmore's command on May 26 and was convinced that "with proper arrangements" the fort could easily be taken

*The last two commanders of Fort Sumter: **above**, Capt. John C. Mitchel, who was killed in July 1864 during the third great bombardment after commanding only two months and 16 days; and **below**, Capt. Thomas A. Huguenin, who remained in charge until Charleston and Fort Sumter were evacuated in February 1865.*

"at any time." The proper arrangements included special light-draught steamers and 1,000-man "assaulting arks" equipped with 51-foot scaling ladders and elevated towers for sharpshooters. Though initial War Department reaction was cool, Foster went ahead with a preliminary operation to complete the demolition of the fort. "Yankee ingenuity" might succeed where routine operations had failed or been judged too costly.

On July 7, 1864, Foster's batteries opened a sustained bombardment against the ruin of Fort Sumter. During the remainder of that month, an average of 350 rounds daily were hurled at the beleagured fort. In some respects, this was the heaviest bombardment Fort Sumter had yet received. Although the gorge ruin was wasted away at one point to within 20 feet of the water, and the shattered sea front was still further reduced, the right face remained erect, its three-gun battery intact; likewise most of the left flank. To Admiral Dahlgren, as late as July 21, the work seemed "nearly impregnable." Debris added to debris, feverish work day and night, and thousands of bags of sand brought from the city by night actually made the fort stronger than ever. If a casemate were breached, it was speedily filled; if the slopes of the ruin invited assault, a bristling array of wooden pikes and barbed-wire entanglements were provided; and there were always the muskets of the 300-man garrison.

The fire slackened in August; Foster's supply of ammunition dwindled, and his requisitions for more went unfulfilled. A scheme for "shaking down" the fort walls by floating down large "powder rafts" failed miserably. Mid-August brought final War Department refusal to supply light-draft steamers; the end of August, sharp disapproval of Foster's "assaulting arks." Meanwhile, Dahlgren had been unwilling to cooperate in an alternate plan of assault and Foster himself was ordered to remain strictly on the defensive. He was also called upon to ship north most of his remaining ammunition and four more regiments of troops to be used in Grant's operations against Richmond.

On September 4, the bombardment begun on July 7 came to an end. In those 61 days, another 14,666 rounds had been hurled against the fort. Sixteen of the garrison had been killed, 65 wounded. On

July 20 Captain Mitchel fell mortally wounded. Capt. Thomas A. Huguenin succeeded him that night.

The last great bombardment of Fort Sumter had taken place. The firing was no more than desultory after September 1864; less than a hundred rounds were hurled at the fort in the months of December and January; none at all in February. During the autumn months it was all Foster's batteries could do to make a reasonable defense of Morris Island, let alone carry on any offensive operations.

In February 1865 the long stalemate came to an end as Gen. William T. Sherman marched north from Savannah through the interior of South Carolina, slicing between the remnants of Gen. John B. Hood's Confederate army on the west and the small Confederate force remaining along the coast. On the 17th, with Sherman in Columbia, Fort Sumter and the other Confederate fortifications in Charleston harbor were quietly evacuated. At 9 o'clock on the morning of the 18th, the United States flag was once more raised over Fort Sumter. The fortunes of war had accomplished what 3,500 tons of metal, a fleet of ironclads, and thousands of men had failed to do.

Maj. Gen. John G. Foster, who replaced Gillmore as commander of land operations at Charleston. Foster had been Anderson's engineer officer at Fort Sumter during the 1861 bombardment.

The 1865 Flag Raising

On April 14, 1865, Robert Anderson, now a retired brigadier general, returned to Fort Sumter to raise again the flag he had pulled down four years before. If he was surprised at the shattered appearance of the fort (shown here in Seth Eastman's companion painting to the one reproduced on pages 4-5), he said nothing, speaking only of the "act of duty" he had come there to perform. "I thank God that I have lived to see this day," he told the throng of spectators and distinguished guests. Then, amid loud applause, he hoisted "to its proper place this flag which floated here during peace, before the first act of this cruel Rebellion."

As the flag rose to the top of the staff and was caught by the breeze from the ocean, "there was one tumultuous shout." The guns of the harbor then thundered in salute. "We raise our fathers' banner, that it may bring back better blessings than those of old," Henry Ward Beecher told the crowd, "that it may cast out the devil of discord; that it may restore lawful government and a prosperity purer and more enduring than that which it protected before; that it may win parted friends from their alienation; that it may inspire hope and inaugurate universal liberty; . . . that it may heal all jealousies, unite all policies, inspire a new national life, compact our strength, purify our principles, ennoble our national ambitions, and make this people great and strong . . . for the peace of the world."

That night, there were fireworks and a full-dress dinner at the Charleston Hotel

hosted by General Gillmore. Speeches and toasts followed one another in quick succession. One of the most moderate and, as events proved, ironic toasts, was given by General Anderson. "I beg you, now," he began, "that you will join me in drinking the health of . . . the man who, when elected President of the United States, was compelled to reach the seat of government without an escort, but a man who now could travel all over our country with millions of hands and hearts to sustain him. I give you the good, the great, the honest man, Abraham Lincoln." Less than an hour later, Abraham Lincoln lay dying on the floor of a Washington theater, an assassin's bullet in his brain.

Part 3

The Fort Today

From Wartime Ruin to National Monument

The task of clearing the rubble and ruin of war from the interior of Fort Sumter began in the 1870s. In the forefront of the project was Quincy A. Gillmore, whose Union gunners were responsible for most of the destruction in the first place. The outer walls of the gorge and right flank, largely demolished by the shellfire, were partially rebuilt. The other walls of the fort, left jagged and torn 30 to 40 feet above the water, were leveled to approximately half their original height. Through a left flank casemate, where a barracks once stood, a new sally port was constructed. Within the fort itself, earth and concrete supports for 10 rifled and smoothbore guns mounted *en barbette* (guns placed on an open parapet) began to take shape.

Construction was well advanced by June 1876, when a shortage of funds forced suspension of activity. By that time, only three permanent barbette platforms had been built; the other seven remained temporary (wooden) platforms upon which were mounted four 8-inch Parrott rifles and two 15-inch Rodman smoothbores. In a modification of the original plan, 11 lower-tier gunrooms of the original fort along the right face and about the salient had been repaired and armed with 6.4-inch Parrotts. These 17 guns, in a gradually deteriorating state, constituted Fort Sumter's armament for the next 23 years.

From 1876 to 1898, the fort stood largely neglected, important mainly as a lighthouse station. Most of that time it was also ungarrisoned and in the charge of a "fortkeeper" or an ordnance sergeant. Lacking maintenance funds, Sumter, even then visited by thousands each year, fell into a state of dilapidation. By 1887 the wooden barbette platforms had rotted away so that "not one gun could be safely fired"; the neat earth slopes had eroded into "irregular mounds"; and quantities of sand had drifted onto the parade ground. At casemate level, salt water dashed freely through the open embrasures, the shutters of which were no longer in working order, and the guns rusted so badly that they could not be moved on their tracks.

By the end of the century, the major world powers were building massive steel navies, and the United States responded by modernizing its coastal defenses. In 1899 two 12-inch breech-loading rifled guns were installed at Fort Sumter, their position further strengthened by earth fill extending to the top of the old walls. The massive concrete emplacement for this battery (named for South Carolinian Isaac Huger, a major general in the American Revolution) dominates the central portion of the fort today. The guns, long since outmoded, were removed for scrap in 1943. During late World War II, Fort Sumter was armed with four 90-mm guns manned by a company of Coast Artillery. The fort, transferred from the War Department to the National Park Service, became a national monument on July 12, 1948.

The following guide highlights the main historical portions of Fort Sumter today. There is no set sequence by which to see the fort, but you may want to refer to the photograph on pages 56-57 for orientation. Hours of operation and tour boat schedules can be ascertained by calling (803) 883-3123.

What to See at Fort Sumter

Sally Port   This present-day entrance to Fort Sumter, runs through the center of the fort's left flank wall. It was built after the Civil War and replaced a gun embrasure. A marker on the left flank near the sally port honors Sumter's Confederate defenders. The original sally port entered through the gorge at the head of a 171-foot stone wharf which once jutted out from the center of the esplanade. The esplanade, a 25½-foot-wide promenade and landing space, extended the full length of the gorge exterior at its base.

Left-Flank Casemates   The first tier of casemates (gunrooms) was surmounted by a second tier identical in appearance. At the time of the April 12, 1861, bombardment these casemates contained several 32-pounders, most of which bore on Fort Johnson. Above the second-tier casemates, guns were mounted *en barbette* on an open terreplein. This arrangement was also used on the fort's right flank and on its right and left faces. Each casemate contained one gun, which could be moved on a track in order to adjust the angle of fire through the embrasure. Fort Sumter was designed for an armament of 135 guns and a garrison of 650 men. There are now two guns mounted on the casemate carriages in the left flank. The one on the left of the sally port is a rifled and banded 42-pounder; the one on the right is a 42-pounder smoothbore. Shielded (by the mass of the gorge) from Federal guns on Morris Island, the left-flank casemates were used as a Confederate headquarters and hospital. The lower half of the outer wall retained its full height until the end of the siege, but was leveled to approximately half this during the 1870s.

Fort Sumter Today

As is clear by comparing the painting on pages 8-9 with the photograph here, Fort Sumter today bears only a superficial resemblance to its original appearance. The multi-tiered work of 1861 was reduced largely to rubble during the Civil War, and Battery Huger, built across the parade ground at the time of the Spanish-American War, dominates the site.

The following labels identify the main features of the present fort. Each is keyed by number to the photograph.

1/Left Face Casemate Ruins
2/Left Flank Casemates
3/Right Face
4/Right Flank
5/Right Gorge Angle
6/Sally Port
7/Parade Ground
8/Union Garrison Monument
9/Powder Magazine
10/Officers' Quarters Ruins
11/Enlisted Men's Barracks
   Ruins
12/Esplanade
13/Granite Wharf Remains
14/12-Pounder Mountain
   Howitzer
15/Battery Huger
16/Museum

Left Face During the 1863-65 siege of Charleston, reverse fire from Union gunners on Morris Island crossed the parade and struck the interior of the left face, destroying the arched brick casemates. Holes caused by these shots, as well as several projectiles themselves, are still visible in the wall. Outside the casemate ruins are two 15-inch smoothbore Rodman guns, an 8-inch Columbiad, and a 10-inch mortar.

Right Face Guns mounted on the lower tier of this face dueled with Fort Moultrie in the initial Confederate attack of 1861. Since the angle of the face allowed it to escape the destructive fire from Federal batteries on Morris Island, its outer wall still stood almost at full height in February 1865. After the destructive bombardments of August 1863, the Confederate garrison mounted three guns in the first-tier casemates just above the right shoulder angle. Referred to as the "Palmetto Battery," because of the protective log cover raised on the exterior, this three-gun position was the sole offensive armament of the fort for several months. All the lower-tier casemates were reclaimed in the 1870s and armed with 100-pounder Parrott rifled cannon. These guns, rusted and worn, were the same type of cannon (and possibly the identical pieces) used by the Federals on Morris Island to bombard Fort Sumter from 1863 to 1865. They were buried with the casemates after Battery Huger was constructed. When the parade ground was excavated in 1959 these casemates were opened and 11 of these Parrott guns were uncovered. They are now displayed in this face.

Right Gorge Angle From a gun in the first-tier casemates, Capt. Abner Doubleday fired the first shot from Fort Sumter on April 12, 1861. This section also sustained the deepest penetration of Confederate shot and shell in the initial attack.

Officers' Quarters A three-story brick building extended the entire length of the gorge (or back wall). In it were quarters for officers, administrative offices, storerooms, powder magazines, and guardhouse. Most of the wooden portions of the building burned during the initial Confederate bombardment in 1861. The small-arms magazine here exploded on December 11, 1863, killing 11 and wounding 41 Confederates. The explosion also tilted the arch over the magazine's entrance. (The effects of that explosion are still visible today.)

Enlisted Men's Barracks Paralleling the left flank casemates, are the ruins of a three-story enlisted men's barracks which originally rose slightly above the fort walls. Another enlisted men's barracks, identical to this one, was on the right flank directly opposite this wall.

Garrison Monument The U.S. Government erected this monument in 1932 "in memory of the garrison defending Fort Sumter during the bombardment of April 12-14, 1861." The tablet contains a roster of the original garrison that served under Major Anderson.

Mountain Howitzer Confederates used several light field pieces, like this 12-pounder mountain howitzer, to defend against a surprise assault by Union infantry troops during the 1863-65 siege.

Other Points of Interest

Fort Moultrie Three different Fort Moultries have occupied this site. The first, a hastily constructed palmetto-log fort, was built in 1776 to protect Charleston against British attack; the second, a five-sided earth and timber fort, was completed in 1798 as part of the new Nation's first organized system of coastal defense; and the third, a more formidable masonry structure begun after the second fort was destroyed by a hurricane in 1804, has remained structurally intact and modified only by the replacement of old weapons with new as technology changed.

During the Civil War, while the struggle for Charleston Harbor centered on Fort Sumter, Fort Moultrie was far from idle and became "a very formidable enemy" to Federal forces. It powerful guns played an important role in the Confederate bombardment of Sumter in 1861. From April 1863 to February 1865, Forts Moultrie and Sumter were the chief defenders of Charleston as repeated Federal land and sea forces hammered at them. "From 1861 to 1865," one historian has written, "Fort Moultrie found itself engaged in perhaps its strangest period of coastal vigilance: defending the Confederate States of America against the United States of America."

The fort today is part of Fort Sumter National Monument and has been restored to interpret the history of nearly 100 years of seacoast defense. From the Harbor Entrance Control Post of World War II the visitor moves steadily backward in time to the exhibit recounting the fateful attack of the British fleet against the first Fort Moultrie in 1776. The visitor center contains a display of artifacts recovered during the restoration. It also provides a film and slide show which documents the proud heritage of coastal fortifications in the United States. The grave of Seminole Chief Osceola, who died a prisoner at Moultrie in 1838, is just outside the sally port. Nearby is a monument listing the Federal sailors who died aboard the monitor *Patapsco*, when it was sunk in Charleston Harbor on January 15, 1865.

Battery Jasper, built adjacent to Fort Moultrie in 1898, is also a part of the national monument. Named in honor of Sergeant Jasper of Revolutionary War fame, this strong seacoast defense work mounted four powerful 10-inch "disappearing" cannon and, though unimpressive in appearance, was infinitely stronger than early masonry structures built to protect Charleston Harbor before the Civil War.

Fort Moultrie is about 10 miles east of Charleston on Sullivan's Island. Follow US 17 north from the city, then take US 17 (business) to Mount Pleasant and turn right onto SC 703. From there follow the signs to the park visitor center across from the fort on Middle Street.

James Island contains the site of Fort Johnson, from which the opening shot of the Civil War was fired on April 12, 1861. All that remains of the fort are an early 19th-century brick powder magazine, a commemorative marker, and traces of the Confederate earthworks of 1863-65. To reach the site, follow US 17 south from Charleston and, after crossing the Ashley River, take the Folly Island turnoff onto Folly Road (SC 171). Proceed 4.7 miles, then turn left onto Fort Johnson Road, which dead ends at the South Carolina Wildlife and Marine Resource Department.

Castle Pinckney, one of the first masonry casemated forts in the United States, was built in 1810. The circular structure, named for Charles Cotesworth Pinckney, a South Carolina Revolutionary War leader, was one of the first Federal installations seized by South Carolina militia on December 27, 1860. Though too far out of range to take part in any of the fighting during the Civil War years, the fort was still a vital link in the Confederate defenses of Charleston. After the war it was maintained as a harbor light station until 1929.

The Battery, or White Point Gardens as it is more formally known, has been a public park since the 1830s and is one of Charleston's most picturesque and historic settings. Soon after the outbreak of the Civil War, Confederate engineers erected huge earthen fortifications here which withstood the shelling of the Union guns mounted on Morris Island. The fortifications were abandoned and the heaviest guns destroyed when Charleston was evacuated in February 1865. The Battery today contains some of the most elegant structures in the city.

For Further Reading

E. Milby Burton, *The Siege of Charleston, 1861-1865.* Columbia: University of South Carolina Press, 1970.

Bruce Catton, *The Coming Fury.* Garden City, N.Y.: Doubleday & Company, 1961.

Peter M. Chaitin & the Editors of Time-Life Books, *The Coastal War: Chesapeake Bay to Rio Grande.* Alexandria, Va.: Time-Life Books, 1984.

Mary Boykin Chesnut, *A Diary From Dixie.* Boston: Houghton Mifflin Company, 1949.

Samuel W. Crawford, *The Genesis of the Civil War: The History of the Fall of Fort Sumter.* New York: J. A. Hill & Company, 1898.

Richard N. Current, *Lincoln and the First Shot.* Philadelphia & New York: J. B. Lippincott Company, 1963.

William C. Davis & the Editors of Time-Life Books, *Brother Against Brother: The War Begins.* Alexandria, Va.: Time-Life Books, 1983.

Abner Doubleday, *Reminiscences of Forts Sumter and Moultrie in 1860-'61.* Spartanburg, S.C.: The Reprint Company, 1976. Originally published in 1876.

Robert U. Johnson & Clarence C. Buel, editors, *Battles and Leaders of the Civil War.* 4 Volumes. New York: Thomas Yoseloff, Inc., 1956. Volumes 1 and 4.

Emanuel Raymond Lewis, *Seacoast Fortifications of the United States: An Introductory History.* Washington, D.C.: Smithsonian Institution Press, 1970.

Kenneth M. Stampp, *And the War Came.* Baton Rouge: Louisiana State University Press, 1950.

Philip Van Doren Stern, compiler, *Prologue to Sumter: The Beginnings of the Civil War from the John Brown Raid to the Surrender of Fort Sumter.* Indianapolis: Indiana University Press, 1961.

W. A. Swanberg, *First Blood: The Story of Fort Sumter.* New York: Charles Scribner's Sons, 1957.

U.S. War Department, *War of the Rebellion: A Compilation of the Official Records of the Union and Confederate Armies.* Washington, D.C.: U.S. Government Printing Office, 1880. Series I, Volumes I, XIV, XXVIII, & XXXV.

☆ GPO: 1984–421-611/10003

Handbook 127

Illustration Credits
Architect of the U.S. Capitol: 4-5, 50-51; Art Commission of the City of New York: 6; William A. Bake: cover, 52-53, 55, 56-57, 58, 59, 61, 62; *Battles and Leaders of the Civil War:* 36 (Dahlgren), 41 (Shaw), 49; *Civil War Times Illustrated:* 14-15; Collection of City Hall, Charleston, S.C.: 12; Fort Sumter National Monument: 16, 26 (Chesnut), 37, 44-45; *Harper's Pictorial History of the Great Rebellion:* 19, 20-21, 22, 23, 25, 35, 38 (Seymour); Kennedy Galleries, Inc., New York: 30-31 (painting); National Park Service: 18 (Floyd), 26, 27, 28, 29, 30-31 (flags), 34, 36 (Gillmore), 38 (Rhett), 40-41 (battle scene), 42, 46, 48, 51 (inset); L. Kenneth Townsend: 8-9.